Manchester United Football Club Quiz Book

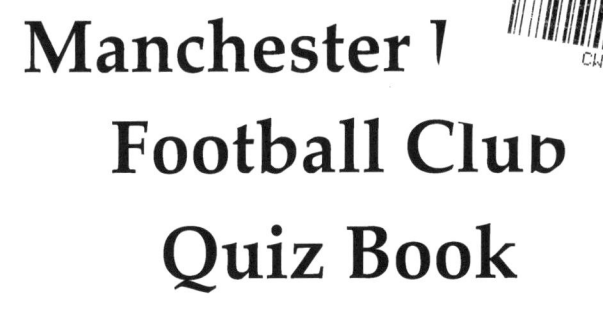

500 TRIVIA QUESTIONS FOR MAN UNITED SUPPORTERS

This Manchester United Football Club quiz book has been extensively researched and has 500 questions about Manchester United Football Club for you to test yourself. The questions are in multiple-choice format and they cover the club's history, honours, records, players, managers, legends and much more. The questions are of varying degrees of difficulty designed to test your knowledge of Man United.

This Manchester United FC Quiz Book is educational, fun and informative and will provide many hours of entertainment for United fans wherever you live.

Copyright © Conan Curtis 2020.

Conan Curtis has asserted his moral right to be identified as the author of this work in accordance with the Copyright Designs and Patents Act 1988. All rights reserved. No part of this book may be reproduced or utilised in any form or by any means, electronic or mechanical, including photocopying, recording or by any information storage and retrieval system, without permission in writing from the author.

Chapter 1: Club History

1. When was United founded?
   a) 1878 b) 1888 c) 1898

2. What were they formed as?
   a) Newton Heath Carriages b) Newton Heath LYR c) Newton Heath Railway

3. What colour was the club's first kit?
   a) Green and gold b) Green and red c) Green and white

4. When did they join the Football League?
   a) 1892 b) 1894 c) 1896

5. When did the club change its name to Manchester United?
   a) 1900 b) 1902 c) 1904

6. What is the club's nickname?
   a) The Devils Advocate b) The Devils in Disguise c) The Red Devils

7. What is the club's official website?
   a) ManU.com b) ManUnited.com c) MUFC.com

8. When was the Munich Air Disaster?
   a) 1954 b) 1956 c) 1958

9. Who is the club's mascot?
   a) Damon the Devil b) Fred the Red c) Redasaurus

10. Where is the training ground?
    a) Barrington b) Carrington c) Warrington

Chapter 1: Answers

1. 1878.
2. Newton Heath LYR Football Club.
3. Green and gold.
4. 1892.
5. 1902.
6. The Red Devils.
7. ManUtd.com
8. 6th February 1958.
9. Fred the Red.
10. Carrington.

Chapter 2: Club Records

11. What is the club's record win in any competition?
    a) 9-0 b) 10-0 c) 11-0

12. What is the club's record win in the Premier League?
    a) 9-0 b) 10-0 c) 11-0

13. What is the club's record unbeaten run in the League?
    a) 23 games b) 26 games c) 29 games

14. What is the most number of goals that United has scored in a league season?
    a) 101 b) 103 c) 105

15. What is the record attendance for a United match?
    a) 101,318 b) 105,318 c) 109,318

16. Who is the oldest player ever to play for United?
    a) Billy Meredith b) Teddy Sheringham c) Edwin van der Sar

17. Who is the youngest ever player to have played for the club?
    a) Angel Gomes b) Mason Greenwood c) Federico Macheda

18. Who is the youngest ever goal scorer for the club?
    a) Mason Greenwood b) Federico Macheda c) Danny Welbeck

19. How many times have United won the League in total – First Division and Premier League?
    a) 16 b) 18 c) 20

20. How many times have United won the FA Cup?
    a) 10 b) 11 c) 12

Chapter 2: Answers

11. 10-0. United beat Anderlecht by this score in a European game on 26th September 1956
12. 9-0. United beat Ipswich by that score on 4th March 1995.
13. 29 games. This happened during the 1998-99 and also in the 2010-11 seasons.
14. 103.
15. 109,318 people saw a match between United and Real Madrid in Michigan in August 2014.
16. Billy Meredith at 46 years 281 days.
17. Angel Gomes.
18. Federico Macheda.
19. 20.
20. 12.

Chapter 3: Players

21. Who has made the appearances for United?
    a) Bobby Charlton b) Ryan Giggs c) Wayne Rooney

22. Who is United's record goal scorer?
    a) Bobby Charlton b) Denis Law c) Wayne Rooney

23. Who has scored the most hat tricks for United?
    a) Denis Law b) Wayne Rooney c) Ruud van Nistelrooy

24. Who was the first United captain to win the League title?
    a) Jack Peddle b) Charlie Roberts c) Harry Stafford

25. Who was the first United Player to win the Ballon d'Or?
    a) George Best b) Bobby Charlton c) Denis Law

26. Who is known as 'La Pioche'?
    a) Patrice Evra b) Anthony Martial c) Paul Pogba

27. Who holds the record for receiving the most red cards?
    a) Phil Jones b) Roy Keane c) John O'Shea

28. Who took out a super injunction to try and prevent being named in relation to an affair with model Imogen Thomas?
    a) Ryan Giggs b) David Moyes c) Dave Sexton

29. How many different team mates did Giggsy have at United?
    a) 130 b) 140 c) 150

30. What is the name of the statue outside the ground featuring Best, Charlton and Law?
    a) One For All b) The Holy Trinity c) The Three Amigos

Chapter 3: Answers

21. Ryan Giggs.
22. Wayne Rooney.
23. Denis Law.
24. Charlie Roberts.
25. Denis Law.
26. Paul Pogba. La Pioche literally means pickaxe.
27. Roy Keane.
28. Ryan Giggs.
29. 150.
30. The Holy Trinity.

Chapter 4: Managers

31. Who is the club's longest serving manager of all time?
    a) Matt Busby b) Tommy Docherty c) Alex Ferguson

32. Who was the club's first manager?
    a) Alfred Albut b) John Bentley c) James West

33. Who was the first manager to win the League?
    a) John Chapman b) Ernest Mangnall c) Jack Robson

34. Who was relieved of his duties by the FA in 1926 for 'improper conduct'?
    a) Herbert Bamlett b) John Chapman c) Clarence Hilditch

35. Who was appointed caretaker manager for five months after the Munich Air Disaster?
    a) Walter Crickmer b) Wilf McGuinness c) Jimmy Murphy

36. Who was the first United manager to be sacked?
    a) Tommy Docherty b) Wilf McGuinness c) Dave Sexton

37. Who was the club's first foreign manager (from outside the UK)?
    a) Louis van Gaal b) Jose Mourinho c) Wilf McGuinness

38. Which club did Bobby Charlton, Darren Ferguson and Brian Kidd all manage?
    a) Peterborough United b) Portsmouth c) Preston North End

39. Who is the only Irish manager in United's history?
    a) Brendan O'Farrell b) Frank O'Farrell c) Paddy O'Farrell

40. Who is the club's most successful manager of all time?
    a) Matt Busby b) Alex Ferguson c) Jose Mourinho

Chapter 4 Answers

31. Alex Ferguson.
32. Alfred Albut who as club secretary in 1892 had responsibility for all team affairs.
33. Ernest Mangnall. He was the first, of many, to win silverware at United by winning the Football League in 1908.
34. John Chapman. After 221 games in charge of United, the FA suspended him from taking part in football management.
35. Jimmy Murphy.
36. Wilf McGuinness.
37. Louis van Gaal.
38. Preston North End.
39. Frank O'Farrell.
40. Sir Alex Ferguson.

Chapter 5: Old Trafford

41. Who designed the ground?
    a) Maxwell Ayrton b) Archibald Leitch c) John Webster
42. When was the stadium inaugurated?
    a) 1900 b) 1910 c) 1920
43. What is the West Stand better known as?
    a) The Shed b) The Shelf c) The Stretford End
44. What is the largest stand at the ground?
    a) East Stand b) Sir Alex Ferguson Stand c) Sir Bobby Charlton Stand
45. How many spectators does the largest stand seat?
    a) 20,000 b) 23,000 c) 26,000
46. What is the size of the pitch?
    a) 104 x 67 metres b) 105 x 68 metres c) 106 x 69 metres
47. How many England international have been played at the ground?
    a) 13 b) 17 c) 21
48. Who did England play in the last international at the stadium?
    a) Greece b) Jamaica c) Spain
49. Who is honoured with a statue on the concourse of the upper tier at the Stretford End?
    a) Tony Dunne b) Ryan Giggs c) Denis Law
50. Who nicknamed the stadium 'The Theatre of Dreams'?
    a) Bobby Charlton b) Bill Foulkes c) Joe Spence

Chapter 5: Answers

41. Archibald Leitch.
42. 1910.
43. The Stretford End.
44. Sir Alex Ferguson Stand.
45. Approximately 26,000.
46. 105 x 68 metres.
47. 17.
48. Spain.
49. Denis Law.
50. Bobby Charlton.

Chapter 5: Club Captains

51. Who was club captain from 1962-1967?
    a) John Aston b) Noel Cantwell c) Paddy Crerand
52. Who was club captain from 1968-1973?
    a) Bobby Charlton b) Bill Foulkes c) Willie Morgan
53. Who was club captain from 1973–1974?
    a) George Graham b) Brian Kidd c) Lou Macari
54. Who was club captain from 1975–1983?
    a) Martin Buchan b) Sammy McIlroy c) Gordon McQueen
55. Who was club captain from 1983-1994?
    a) Remi Moses b) Bryan Robson c) Gordon Strachan
56. Who was club captain from 1994-1996?
    a) Steve Bruce b) Paul Ince c) Gary Pallister
57. Who was club captain from 1997-2005?
    a) Roy Keane b) David May c) Paul Scholes
58. Who was club captain from 2005-2011?
    a) Wes Brown b) Rio Ferdinand c) Gary Neville
59. Who was club captain from 2011-2014?
    a) Darren Fletcher b) Nemanja Vidic c) Ashley Young
60. Who was club captain from 2014-2017?
    a) Marouane Fellaini b) Wayne Rooney c) Antonio Valencia

Chapter 6: Answers

51. Noel Cantwell.
52. Bobby Charlton.
53. George Graham.
54. Martin Buchan.
55. Bryan Robson.
56. Steve Bruce.
57. Roy Keane.
58. Gary Neville.
59. Nemanja Vidic.
60. Wayne Rooney.

Chapter 7: Sir Matt Busby Player of The Season Award

61. Who won the Player of the season award for 2019-20?
    a) Bruno Fernandes b) Nemanja Matic c) Marcus Rashford
62. Who won the Player of the season award for 2018-19?
    a) Victor Lindelöf b) Paul Pogba c) Luke Shaw
63. Who won the Player of the season award for 2017-18?
    a) Eric Bailly b) David de Gea c) Anthony Martial
64. Who won the Player of the season award for 2016-17?
    a) Ander Herrera b) Marcos Rojo c) Zlatan Ibrahimović
65. Who won the Player of the season award for 2015-16?
    a) Michael Carrick b) David de Gea c) Juan Mata
66. Who won the Player of the season award for 2014-15?
    a) Daley Blind b) David de Gea c) Angle di Maria
67. Who won the Player of the season award for 2013-14?
    a) Rio Ferdinand b) David de Gea c) Patrice Evra
68. Who won the Player of the season award for 2012-13?
    a) Darren Fletcher b) Jesse Lingard c) Robin van Persie
69. Who won the Player of the season award for 2011-12?
    a) Michael Owen b) Ji-Sung Park c) Antonio Valencia
70. Who won the Player of the season award for 2010-11?
    a) Javier Hernandez b) Edwin van der Saar c) Nemanja Vidic

Chapter 7: Answers

61. Bruno Fernandes.
62. Luke Shaw.
63. David de Gea.
64. Ander Herrera.
65. David de Gea.
66. David de Gea.
67. David de Gea.
68. Robin van Persie.
69. Antonio Valencia.
70. Javier Hernandez.

Chapter 8: Shirt Numbers

71. What shirt number is associated with Bobby Charlton?
    a) 7 b) 8 c) 9
72. What shirt number is associated with Paul Scholes?
    a) 8 b) 18 c) 28
73. What shirt number is associated with Pat Crerand?
    a) 3 b) 4 c) 5
74. What shirt number is associated with Nobby Stiles?
    a) 2 b) 6 c) 11
75 What shirt number is associated with Paul Pogba?
    a) 4 b) 5 c) 6
76. What shirt number is associated with Phil Jones?
    a) 4 b) 5 c) 6
77. What shirt number is associated with Michael Carrick?
    a) 6 b) 10 c) 16
78. What shirt number is associated with Park ji-Sung?
    a) 11 b) 13 c) 15
79. What shirt number is associated with Lou Macari?
    a) 6 b) 8 c) 10
80. What shirt number is associated with Juan Mata?
    a) 6 b) 8 c) 10

Chapter 8: Answers

71. Charlton – 9.
72. Scholes -18.
73. Crerand – 4.
74. Stiles – 6.
75. Pogba – 6.
76. Jones – 4.
77. Carrick -16.
78. ji-Sung – 13.
79. Macari – 10.
80. Mata – 8.

Chapter 9: Nationalities

81. Where was Antonio Valencia born?
    a) Colombia b) Ecuador c) Venezuela

82. Where was Mikael Silvestre born?
    a) Belgium b) France c) Spain

83. Where was Clayton Blackmore born?
    a) Ireland b) Scotland c) Wales

84. Where was Marcos Rojo born?
    a) Argentina b) Brazil c) Uruguay

85. Where was Marouane Fellaini born?
    a) Belgium b) Belize c) Brazil

86. Where was Peter Schmeichel born?
    a) Denmark b) Norway c) Sweden

87. Where was Norman Whiteside born?
    a) New Zealand b) Northern Ireland c) Norway

88. Where was Park Ji-sung born?
    a) China b) Japan c) South Korea

89. Where was Gary Bailey born?
    a) England b) South Africa c) Wales

90. Where was Jesper Olsen born?
    a) Denmark b) Norway c) Sweden

Chapter 9: Answers

81. Valencia was born in Ecuador.
82. Silvestre was born in France.
83. Blackmore was born in Wales.
84. Rojo was born in Argentina.
85. Fellaini was born in Belgium.
86. Schmeichel was born in Denmark.
87. Whiteside was born in Northern Ireland.
88. Ji-sung was born in South Korea.
89. Bailey was born in England.
90. Olsen was born in Denmark.

Chapter 10: Ole Gunnar Solskjaer

91. Where was Solskjaer born?
    a) Denmark b) Norway c) Sweden

92. When did he make his debut as a player for United?
    a) 1994 b) 1996 c) 1998

93. What position did he play?
    a) Defence b) Midfield c) Forward

94. How many games did he play for United?
    a) 333 b) 366 c) 399

95. When did he become manager at United?
    a) 2017 b) 2018 c) 2019

96. What was the last he managed before United?
    a) Cardiff City b) Molde c) Wrexham

97. How many games in a row did United win after he became manager?
    a) 3 b) 4 c) 5

98. Where did United finish at the end of his first season in charge (2018-19)?
    a) 4th b) 6th c) 8th

99. Who was the first player he bought for United?
    a) Daniel James b) Harry Maguire c) Aaron Wan-Bissaka

100. How many semi-finals did United reach during his first full season in charge (2019-20)?
    a) 1 b) 2 c) 3

Chapter 10: Answers

91. Norway.
92. 1996.
93. Forward.
94. 366.
95. He was appointed caretaker manager in December 2018. He was appointed manager on a permanent basis in March 2019.
96. Molde.
97. 5.
98. 6th.
99. Daniel James.
100. 3. The League Cup semi-final, the FA Cup semi-final and the Europa League semi-final.

Chapter 11: Jose Mourinho

101. Where was Mourinho born?
    a) Madeira b) Portugal c) The Azores

102. What position did he play?
    a) Defence b) Midfield c) Attack

103. When did he become manager at United?
    a) 2015 b) 2016 c) 2017

104. Prior to joining United, how many Champions League trophies had he won as manager?
    a) 1 b) 2 c) 3

105. Prior to joining United, how many English clubs had he managed?
    a) 1 b) 2 c) 3

106. Prior to joining United, how many Premier League titles had he won as manager?
    a) 1 b) 2 c) 3

107. Who was the first player he bought for United?
    a) Eric Bailly b) Zlatan Ibrahimovic c) Henrikh Mkhitaryan

108. Where did United finish at the end of his first season in charge?
    a) 4th b) 6th c) 8th

109. How many trophies titles did he win as United manager?
    a) 0 b) 1 c) 2

110. How many games was he in charge of United?
    a) 114 b) 144 c) 174

Chapter 11: Answers

101. He was born in Setubal, Portugal.
102. Midfield.
103. 27th May 2016.
104. 2 – with Porto and Inter Milan.
105. 1 – Chelsea.
106. 3.
107. Eric Bailly.
108. 6th.
109. Under Mourinho's management, the club won the Community Shield and the Europa League.
110. 144.

Chapter 12: Louis van Gaal

111. Where was van Gaal born?
    a) Amsterdam b) Edam c) Rotterdam

112. What position did he play during his playing career?
    a) Defence b) Midfield c) Attack

113. How many League titles had he won prior to joining United?
    a) 3 b) 5 c) 7

114. Who did he manage just before coming to United?
    a) Barcelona b) Bayern Munich c) The Netherlands national team

115. What year did he become manager of United?
    a) 2012 b) 2013 c) 2014

116. Who was his first signing for United?
    a) Daley Blind b) Ander Herrera c) Marcos Rojo

117. Where did the club finish at the end of his first season in charge?
    a) 3rd b) 4th c) 5th

118. What was the only trophy he won with United?
    a) Europa League b) FA Cup c) League Cup

119. How many games was he in charge of United?
    a) 103 b) 133 c) 163

120. What was his last game in charge of United?
    a) Charity Shield b) FA Cup Final c) League Cup Final

Chapter 12: Answers

111. Amsterdam.
112. Midfield.
113. 7 in total – 4 in the Netherlands, 2 in Spain and 1 in Germany.
114. The Netherlands National team, which he coached to the Word Cup semi final just before joining United.
115. 2014.
116. Daley Blind.
117. 4th.
118. FA Cup.
119. 103.
120. FA Cup Final on 21st May 2016.

Chapter 13: Ron Atkinson

121. Where was Atkinson born?
    a) Leeds b) Leicester c) Liverpool

122. What position did he play during his playing career?
    a) Defence b) Midfield c) Attack

123. How was his nickname as a player?
    a) The Brute b) The Tanks c) The Wall

124. Who did he manage just before coming to United?
    a) Aston Villa b) Cambridge United c) WBA

125. What year did he become manager of United?
    a) 1981 b) 1982 c) 1983

126. Who was his first signing for United?
    a) Remi Moses b) Bryan Robson c) Frank Stapleton

127. Where did the club finish at the end of his first season in charge?
    a) 3rd b) 6th c) 9th

128. How many games was he in charge of United?
    a) 192 b) 292 c) 392

129. How many FA Cups did United win in total under Big Ron?
    a) 1 b) 2 c) 3

130. Which TV channel did he join as a co-commentator in the 1990s?
    a) BBC b) Sky Sports c) ITV Sport

Chapter 13: Answers

121. Liverpool.
122. Midfield. He played in what used to be called a 'Wing Half'.
123. The Tank.
124. WBA.
125. 1981.
126. Frank Stapleton.
127. 3rd.
128. 192.
129. 2.
130. ITV Sport.

Chapter 14: Sir Matt Busby

131. Where was Busby born?
 a) Northern Ireland b) Scotland c) Wales

132. What position did he play?
 a) Right Half b) Centre Half c) Left Half

133. When did he become United manager?
 a) 1945 b) 1946 c) 1947

134. Where did United finish at the end of his first season in charge?
 a) 2nd b) 5th c) 8th

135. Which Olympics did he manage the Great Britain side?
 a) 1948 b) 1952 c) 1956

136. Who offered him the manager's job in 1956?
 a) Bayern Munich b) Juventus c) Real Madrid

137. Who was Busby's final signing at United?
 a) Sammy McIlroy b) Willie Morgan c) Ian Ure

138. How many League titles did he win at United?
 a) 3 b) 4 c) 5

139. How many trophies did he win in total at United?
 a) 9 b) 11 c) 13

140. How many games was he in charge of United?
 a) 941 b) 1041 c) 1141

Chapter 14: Answers

131. Busby was born in Scotland.
132. Right Half. He played over 300 games for Manchester city and Liverpool.
133. 1945.
134. 2nd.
135. 1948.
136. Real Madrid.
137. Sammy McIlroy.
138. 5.
139. 13.
140. 1141.

Chapter 15: Champions League 2007–08

141. Who did United beat 2-1 on aggregate in the round of 16?
    a) Lens b) Lille c) Lyon

142. Who did United beat 3-0 on aggregate in the quarter-final?
    a) Inter Milan b) Juventus c) Roma

143. Who did United beat 1-0 on aggregate in the semi-final?
    a) Barcelona b) Real Madrid c) Seville

144. Where was the final played?
    a) London b) Moscow c) Rome

145. Who did United beat in the final?
    a) Arsenal b) Chelsea c) Liverpool

146. Who scored United's goal during normal time?
    a) Wayne Rooney b) Cristiano Ronaldo c) Carlos Tevez

147. What was the score on penalties?
    a) 4-3 b) 5-4 c) 6-5

148. Who unluckily slipped when his penalty could have won the trophy for Chelsea?
    a) Didier Drogba b) Frank Lampard c) John Terry

149. Whose penalty kick was saved by Edin van der Sar to win the trophy for United?
    a) Nicolas Anelka b) Florent Malouda c) Salomon Kalou

150. Who was the captain who lifted the trophy?
    a) Rio Ferdinand b) Owen Hargreaves c) Nemanja Vidic

Chapter 15: Answers

141. Lyon.
142. Roma.
143. Barcelona.
144. Moscow.
145. Chelsea.
146. Cristiano Ronaldo.
147. 6-5.
148. John Terry.
149. Nicolas Anelka.
150. Rio Ferdinand.

Chapter 16: Champions League 1998-99

151. Who did United beat 2-0 on aggregate in the qualifying round?
    a) Lazio b) Lille c) LKS Lodz

152. Who did United finish second to in the group stage?
    a) Bayer Kitzingen b) Bayer Leverkusen c) Bayern Munich

153. Who did United beat 3-1 on aggregate in the quarter-final?
    a) Fiorentina b) Inter Milan c) Roma

154. Who did United beat 4-3 on aggregate in the semi-final?
    a) AC Milan b) Juventus c) Sampdoria

155. Where was the final played?
    a) Barcelona b) Madrid c) Valencia

156. Who did United beat in the final?
    a) AC Milan b) Bayern Munich c) Real Madrid

157. What was the score?
    a) 2-0 b) 2-1 c) 3-1

158. Who scored the first goal?
    a) David Beckham b) Teddy Sheringham c) Ole Gunnar Solskjaer

159. Who scored the winning goal?
    a) Teddy Sheringham b) Ole Gunnar Solskjaer c) Dwight Yorke

160. Who was the captain who lifted the trophy?
    a) Roy Keane b) Gary Neville c) Peter Schmeichel

Chapter 16: Answers

151. LKS Lodz.
152. Bayern Munich,
153. Inter Milan.
154. Juventus. After drawing the home leg 1-1, United won the return leg 3-2 in a memorable match in Turin.
155. Barcelona.
156. Bayern Munich.
157. 2-1.
158. Teddy Sheringham.
159. Ole Gunnar Solskjaer.
160. Peter Schmeichel.

Chapter 17: European Cup 1968

161. Which country were Hibernians, United's opponents in the first round from?
    a) Malta b) Moldova c) Montenegro

162. Who did United beat 2-1 on aggregate in the second round?
    a) Sarajevo b) Sivasspor c) St. Etienne

163. Who did United beat 2-1 on aggregate in the quarter-final?
    a) Gornik Zabrze b) Legia Warsaw c) Slask Wroclaw

164. Who did United beat 4-3 on aggregate in the semi-final?
    a) Athletic Bilbao b) Barcelona c) Real Madrid

165. Where was the final played?
    a) Athens b) London c) Paris

166. Who did United beat in the final?
    a) Benfica b) Sporting Lisbon c) Porto

167. Who scored United's goal in the 1-1 draw during normal time?
    a) Bobby Charlton b) George Best c) Brian Kidd

168. Who was the United goalkeeper in the final?
    a) Harry Gregg b) Jimmy Rimmer c) Alex Stepney

169. What colour shirts did United wear in the final?
    a) Red b) White c) Blue

170. Who was the captain who lifted the trophy?
    a) John Aston b) Bobby Charlton c) Tony Dunne

Chapter 17: Answers

161. Malta.
162. Sarajevo.
163. Gornik Zabrze.
164. Real Madrid.
165. Wembley Stadium, London.
166. Benfica.
167. Bobby Charlton.
168. Alex Stepney.
169. Blue.
170. Bobby Charlton.

Chapter 18: European Cup Winner's Cup 1990-91

171. Which Hungarian team did United beat 3-0 on aggregate in the first round?
    a) Debrecen b) Honved c) Pecsi Mecsek

172. Who did United beat 5-0 on aggregate in the second round?
    a) Cardiff City b) Swansea City c) Wrexham

173. Who did United beat 3-1 on aggregate in the quarter-final?
    a) Marseille b) Monaco c) Montpellier

174. Who did United beat 4-2 on aggregate in the semi-final?
    a) Dynamo Kiev b) Legia Warsaw c) Standard Liege

175. Where was the final played?
    a) Riga b) Rome c) Rotterdam

176. Who did United beat in the final?
    a) Barcelona b) Real Madrid c) Valencia

177. What was the score?
    a) 1-0 b) 2-0 c) 2-1

178. Who scored the first goal?
    a) Clayton Blackmore b) Mark Hughes c) Brian McClair

179. How many of the starting eleven were English?
    a) 3 b) 5 c) 7

180. Who was the captain who lifted the trophy?
    a) Steve Bruce b) Paul Ince c) Bryan Robson

Chapter 18: Answers

171. Pecsi Mecsek.
172. Wrexham.
173. Montpellier.
174. Legia Warsaw.
175. Rotterdam.
176. Barcelona.
177. 2-1.
178. Mark Hughes scored both of United's goals.
179. 7 of the starting line-up were English.
180. Bryan Robson.

Chapter 19: Europa League 2016-17

181. Who did United finish second to in the group stage?
    a) Besiktas b) Fenerbahce c) Galatasaray

182. Who did United beat 2-1 on aggregate in the Round of 16?
    a) RB Salzburg b) Roma c) Rostov

183. Who did United beat 3-2 on aggregate in the quarter-final?
    a) Anderlecht b) Antwerp c) Genk

184. Who did United beat 2-1 on aggregate in the semi-final?
    a) Real Betis b) Celta Vigo c) Sevilla

185. Where was the final played?
    a) Barcelona b) London c) Stockholm

186. Who did United beat in the final?
    a) Ajax b) Feyenoord c) PSV Eindhoven

187. What was the score?
    a) 1-0 b) 2-0 c) 2-1

188. Who scored the first goal?
    a) Henrikh Mkhitaryan b) Paul Pogba c) Marcus Rashford

189. How many of the starting eleven were English?
    a) 1 b) 2 c) 3

190. Who was the captain who lifted the trophy?
    a) Juan Mata b) Wayne Rooney c) Antonio Valencia

Chapter 19: Answers

181. Fenerbahce.
182. Rostov.
183. Anderlecht.
184. Celta Vigo.
185. Stockholm.
186. Ajax.
187. 2-0.
188. Mkhitaryan.
189. Two Englishmen started the match – Chris Smalling and Marcus Rashford.
190. Although Antonio Valencia started as captain on the night, substitute and club captain Wayne Rooney lifted the trophy.

Chapter 20: Premier League 2012-13

191. How many points did United finish the season with?
    a) 87 b) 88 c) 89

192. Which team finished second?
    a) Aston Villa b) Blackburn Rovers c) Norwich City

193. What was the points difference between first and second?
    a) 5 b) 8 c) 11

194. How many goals were scored during the season?
    a) 67 b) 77 c) 87

195. Who was United's leading goal scorer?
    a) Javier Hernandez b) Robin van Persie c) Danny Welbeck

196. How many goals did the leading scorer score in the League?
    a) 20 b) 23 c) 26

197. Who was the last home game of the season against (and Fergie's last ever home game)?
    a) Aston Villa b) Chelsea c) Swansea City

198. What was the score in the last game of the season – at WBA (and Fergie's last ever game in charge)?
    a) 3-3 b) 4-4 c) 5-5

199. How many players were used in total during the season?
    a) 21 b) 23 c) 25

200. How many League titles have United now won?
    a) 18 b) 19 c) 20

Chapter 20: Answers

191. 89 points.
192. Manchester City.
193. 11.
194. 86.
195. Robin van Persie.
196. 26.
197. Swansea City. A 2-1 victory for United preceded the medals being handed out and an emotional spine-tingling farewell to Sir Alex.
198. 5-5.
199. 25.
200. 20. An English record which stands to this day.

Chapter 21: Premier League 2007-08

201. How many points did United finish the season with?
   a) 87 b) 88 c) 89

202. Which team finished second?
   a) Arsenal b) Chelsea c) Liverpool

203. What was the points difference between first and second?
   a) 1 b) 2 c) 3

204. How many goals were scored during the season?
   a) 80 b) 85 c) 90

205. Who was United's leading goal scorer?
   a) Cristiano Ronaldo b) Wayne Rooney c) Carlos Tevez

206. How many goals did the leading scorer score in the League?
   a) 21 b) 26 c) 31

207. Which goalkeeper made just one appearance during the season?
   a) Ben Foster b) Tom Heaton c) Tomasz Kuszczak

208. How many clean-sheets did the club keep during the season?
   a) 17 b) 19 c) 21

209. Who did United beat on penalties in the 2007 Community Shield pre-season curtain raiser?
   a) Arsenal b) Chelsea c) Portsmouth

210. How many players were used in total during the season?
   a) 21 b) 23 c) 25

Chapter 21: Answers

201. 87 points.
202. Chelsea.
203. 2.
204. 80.
205. Cristiano Ronaldo.
206. 31.
207. Ben Foster.
208. 21, including 6 in a row.
209. Chelsea.
210. 25.

Chapter 22: Premier League 1998-99

211. How many points did United finish the season with?
    a) 79 b) 81 c) 83

212. Which team finished second?
    a) Arsenal b) Chelsea c) Leeds United

213. What was the points difference between first and second?
    a) 1 b) 2 c) 3

214. How many goals were scored during the season?
    a) 70 b) 75 c) 80

215. Who was United's leading goal scorer in the League?
    a) Andy Cole b) Ole Gunnar Solskjaer c) Dwight Yorke

216. How many goals did the leading scorer score in the League?
    a) 18 b) 21 c) 24

217. How many clean-sheets did the club keep during the season?
    a) 11 b) 12 c) 13

218. How many players were used in total during the season?
    a) 21 b) 22 c) 23

219. Who did United beat 8-1 away from home in their biggest win of the season?
    a) Charlton Athletic b) Nottingham Forest c) Wimbledon

220. Who did United beat 2-1 in the last game of the season to clinch the title?
    a) Arsenal b) Chelsea c) Tottenham Hotspur

Chapter 22: Answers

211. 79.
212. Arsenal.
213. 1 point.
214. 80.
215. Dwight Yorke.
216. 18.
217. 13.
218. 23.
219. Nottingham Forest.
220. Tottenham Hotspur.

Chapter 23: Premier League 1992-93

221. How many points did United finish the season with?
    a) 80 b) 84 c) 88

222. Which team finished second?
    a) Aston Villa b) Blackburn Rovers c) Norwich City

223. What was the points difference between first and second?
    a) 6 b) 8 c) 10

224. How many goals were scored during the season?
    a) 67 b) 77 c) 87

225. Who was United's leading goal scorer?
    a) Eric Cantona b) Mark Hughes c) Brian McClair

226. How many goals did the leading scorer score in the League?
    a) 11 b) 15 c) 19

227. Who was the club's crucial signing in November 1992?
    a) Eric Cantona b) Dion Dublin c) Les Sealey

228. How many players were used in total during the season?
    a) 20 b) 24 c) 28

229. Who did United beat 5-0 in the biggest home win of the season?
    a) Coventry City b) Middlesbrough c) Oldham Athletic

230. How many of the last seven matches of the season did United win?
    a) 3 b) 5 c) 7

Chapter 23: Answers

221. 84 points.
222. Aston Villa.
223. 10.
224. 67.
225. Mark Hughes.
226. 15.
227. Eric Cantona.
228. 20.
229. Coventry City.
230. All seven.

Chapter 24: First Division 1951-52

231. How many points did United finish the season with (two point for a win)?
    a) 51 b) 54 c) 57

232. Which team finished second?
    a) Arsenal b) Portsmouth c) Tottenham Hotspur

233. What was the points difference between first and second?
    a) 2 b) 3 c) 4

234. How many goals were scored during the season?
    a) 75 b) 85 c) 95

235. Who was United's leading goal scorer?
    a) Roger Byrne b) Stan Pearson c) Jack Rowley

236. How many goals did the leading scorer score in the League?
    a) 20 b) 25 c) 30

237. Who was the captain who lifted the trophy?
    a) Johnny Berry b) Johnny Carey c) Henry Cockburn

238. How many clean-sheets did the club keep during the season?
    a) 6 b) 8 c) 10

239. Who did United beat 6-1 in the last game of the season?
    a) Arsenal b) Chelsea c) Tottenham Hotspur

240. How many players were used in total during the season?
    a) 20 b) 22 c) 24

Chapter 24: Answers

231. 54.
232. Tottenham Hotspur.
233. 4.
234. 95.
235. Jack Rowley.
236. 30.
237. Johnny Carey.
238. 10.
239. Arsenal.
240. 24.

Chapter 25: FA Cup 2016

241. Who did United beat 1-0 at home in the third round?
a) Leeds United b) Rotherham United c) Sheffield United

242. Who did United beat 3-1 away in the fourth round?
a) Darlington b) Derby County c) Doncaster Rovers

243. Who did United beat 3-0 away in the fifth round?
a) Ipswich Town b) Mansfield Town c) Shrewsbury Town

244. Who did United need to beat in a replay in the sixth round?
a) Leeds United b) Newcastle United c) West Ham United

245. Who did United beat 2-1 in the semi-final?
a) Arsenal b) Blackburn Rovers c) Everton

246. Who did United beat in the final?
a) Chelsea b) Crystal Palace c) Millwall

247. What was the score (after extra time)?
a) 1-0 b) 2-1 c) 3-2

248. Who scored the winner in extra time?
a) Jesse Lingard b) Anthony Martial c) Juan Mata

249. How did he score the goal?
a) Right foot shot b) Left foot shot c) Header

250. Who was the captain who lifted the trophy?
a) Wayne Rooney b) Antonio Valencia c) Ashley Young

Chapter 25: Answers

241. Sheffield United.
242. Derby County.
243. Shrewsbury Town.
244. West Ham United.
245. Everton.
246. Crystal Place.
247. 2-1 after extra time, after the scores had finished 1-1 after 90 minutes.
248. Jesse Lingard.
249. Right foot.
250. Wayne Rooney.

Chapter 26: FA Cup 1999

251. What score did United beat Middlesbrough in the third round?
    a) 3-1 b) 4-1 c) 5-1

252. What score did United beat Liverpool in the third round?
    a) 1-0 b) 2-1 c) 3-2

253. Who did United beat 1-0 in the fifth round?
    a) Brentford b) Charlton c) Fulham

254. Who scored both goals in the 2-0 replay win over Chelsea in the sixth round?
    a) Henning Berg b) Andy Cole c) Dwight Yorke

255. What score did United beat Arsenal in a famous semi-final replay art Villa Park?
    a) 1-0 b) 2-1 c) 3-2

256. Who did United beat in the final?
    a) Leeds United b) Newcastle United c) West Ham United

257. What was the score?
    a) 2-0 b) 3-0 c) 4-0

258. Who scored the first goal?
    a) David Beckham b) Paul Scholes c) Teddy Sheringham

259. Who scored the second goal?
    a) David Beckham b) Paul Scholes c) Teddy Sheringham

260. Who was the captain who lifted the trophy?
    a) Roy Keane b) David May c) Gary Neville

Chapter 26 – Answers

251. 3-1.
252. 2-1.
253. Fulham.
254. Dwight Yorke.
255. 2-1.
256. Newcastle United.
257. 2-0.
258. Teddy Sheringham.
259. Paul Scholes.
260. Roy Keane.

Chapter 27: FA Cup 1977

261. What score did United beat Walsall in the third round?
    a) 1-0 b) 3-0 c) 5-0

262. What score did United beat QPR in the third round?
    a) 1-0 b) 3-0 c) 5-0

263. Who did United need to beat in a replay in the fifth round?
    a) Southampton b) Southport c) Sunderland

264. Who did United beat in the sixth round?
    a) Aldershot b) Arsenal c) Aston Villa

265. Who did United beat 2-1 in the semi-final?
    a) Arsenal b) Blackburn Rovers c) Everton

266. Who did United beat in the final?
    a) Crystal Palace b) Everton c) Liverpool

267. What was the score?
    a) 1-0 b) 2-1 c) 3-2

268. Who scored the winning goal?
    a) Jimmy Greenhoff b) Gordon Hill c) Stuart Pearson

269. Who was the manager?
    a) Ron Atkinson b) Tommy Docherty c) Dave Sexton

270. Who was the captain who lifted the trophy?
    a) Martin Buchan b) Brian Greenhoff c) Jimmy Nicholl

Chapter 27 – Answers

261. 1-0.
262. 1-0.
263. Southampton.
264. Aston Villa.
265. Leeds United.
266. Liverpool.
267. 2-1.
268. Jimmy Greenhoff.
269. Tommy Docherty.
270. Martin Buchan.

Chapter 28: David de Gea

271. Where was de Gea born?
    a) Madrid b) Malaga c) Marbella

272. How tall is he?
    a) 6 feet 2 inches b) 6 feet 4 inches c) 6 feet 6 inches

273. Which club did United buy him from?
    a) Athletic Bilbao b) Atletico Levante c) Atletico Madrid

274. What transfer fee did United pay for him?
    a) £16.9 million b) £ 18.9 million c) £20.9 million

275. How old was he when he made his first team debut for United?
    a) 20 b) 21 c) 22

276. How old was he when he made his international debut for Spain?
    a) 21 b) 22 c) 23

277. When did he win the Premier League Golden Glove?
    a) 2015-16 b) 2016-17 c) 2017-18

278. How many times has he won the Matt Busby Player of The Year Award?
    a) 2 b) 3 c) 4

279. How many times has he won the Match of the Day Save of the Season award?
    a) 1 b) 3 c) 5

280. What is his nickname?
    a) Safe Hands b) Sticky Gloves c) The Panther

Chapter 28: Answers

271. Madrid.
272. 6 feet 4 inches.
273. Atletico Madrid.
274. £18.9 million.
275. 21.
276. 23.
277. 2017-18.
278. 4.
279. 5.
280. Sticky Gloves.

Chapter 29: Wayne Rooney

281. Where was Rooney born?
   a) Merseyside b) Middlesex c) Midlothian

282. Which club did United buy him from?
   a) Derby County b) Everton c) Wolves

283. What transfer fee did United pay for him?
   a) £15.6 million b) £ 20.6 million c) £25.6 million

284. How old was he when he made his first team debut for United?
   a) 17 b) 18 c) 19

285. How many appearances did he make for United?
   a) 519 b) 539 c) 559

286. How many goals did he score for United?
   a) 223 b) 253 c) 283

287. When did he win the PFA Players' Player of the Year Award?
   a) 2007-08 b) 2009-10 c) 2011-12

288. What is his nickname?
   a) Pit Bull b) Roo c) Wazza

289. How many England caps did he win?
   a) 100 b) 110 c) 120

290. Which MLS side did he play for in 2018?
   a) DC United b) LA Galaxy c) New York Red Bulls

Chapter 29: Answers

281. He was born in Liverpool, Merseyside.
282. Everton.
283. £25.6 million
284. Aged 19, he scored a hat-trick on his debut.
285. 559.
286. 253.
287. 2009-10.
288. All three have been used as his nicknames, although Wazza was the most common nickname used by his teammates.
289. 120.
290. DC United.

Chapter 30: Ruud Van Nistelrooy

291. Where was van Nistelrooy born?
 a) Belgium b) Luxembourg c) The Netherlands

292. Which club did United buy him from?
 a) Ajax b) Feyenoord c) PSV Eindhoven

293. What transfer fee did United pay for him?
 a) £15 million b) £17 million c) £19 million

294. How old was he when he made his first team debut for United?
 a) 22 b) 24 c) 26

295. Who did he score against on his debut?
 a) Arsenal b) Liverpool c) Manchester City

296. How many appearances did he make for United?
 a) 219 b) 249 c) 279

297. How many goals did he score for United?
 a) 130 b) 140 c) 150

298. When did he win the PFA Players' Player of the Year Award?
 a) 2001-02 b) 2002-03 c) 2003-04

299. Which season did he win the Premier League Golden Boot award?
 a) 2001-02 b) 2002-03 c) 2003-04

300. Which club did he move to after United?
 a) Ajax b) Juventus c) Real Madrid

Chapter 30: Answers

291. The Netherlands.
292. PSV.
293. £19 million.
294. 24.
295. Ruud scored on his debut against Liverpool in the 2001 FA Charity Shield.
296. 219.
297. 150.
298. 2001-02.
299. 2002-03.
300. Real Madrid.

Chapter 31: Roy Keane

301. Where was Keane born?
    a) Cork b) Galway c) Limerick

302. Which club did United buy him from?
    a) Celtic b) Cobh Ramblers c) Nottingham Forest

303. What transfer fee did United pay for him?
    a) £1.75 million b) £ 3.75 million c) £5.75 million

304. How old was he when he made his first team debut for United?
    a) 21 b) 22 c) 23

305. How many appearances did he make for United?
    a) 420 b) 450 c) 480

306. How many goals did he score for United?
    a) 31 b) 41 c) 51

307. How many Premier League titles did he win with United?
    a) 5 b) 6 c) 7

308. Which club did he move to after United?
    a) Aberdeen b) Celtic c) Rangers

309. What was the first team he managed?
    a) Aston Villa b) Ipswich Town c) Sunderland

310. What was the title of his first autobiography?
    a) Keane: My Life b) Keane: The Autobiography c) The First Half

Chapter 31: Answers

301. Cork.
302. Nottingham Forest.
303. £3.75 million which was a British transfer record at the time.
304. 21. He made his debut two days before his 22nd birthday.
305. 480.
306. 51.
307. 7.
308. Celtic.
309. Sunderland.
310. Keane: The Autobiography.

Chapter 32: Paul Scholes

311. Where was Scholes born?
    a) Salford b) Stoke c) Sunderland

312. How tall is he?
    a) 5 feet 6 inches b) 5 feet 8 inches c) 5 feet 10 inches

313. How old was he when he made his first team debut?
    a) 17 b) 18 c) 19

314. What position did he normally play?
    a) Defence b) Midfield c) Attack

315. How many appearances did he make in total for the club?
    a) 618 b) 668 c) 718

316. How many goals did he score for the club?
    a) 46 b) 66 c) 86

317. How many international caps did he win?
    a) 46 b) 56 c) 66

318. How many Premier League titles did he win at the club?
    a) 7 b) 9 c) 11

319. Who were the opposition for his testimonial match in 2011?
    a) New York City b) New York Cosmos c) New York Red Bulls

320. What was the title of his autobiography?
    a) Scholes: My Career b) Scholes: My Life c) Scholes: My Story

Chapter 32: Answers

311. Salford.
312. 5 feet 6 inches tall.
313. 19.
314. Midfield.
315. 718.
316. 155.
317. 66.
318. 11.
319. New York Cosmos.
320. Scholes: My Story.

Chapter 33: Gary Neville

321. Where was Neville born?
    a) Blackburn b) Bolton c) Bury

322. How tall is he?
    a) 5 feet 9 inches b) 5 feet 10 inches c) 5 feet 11 inches

323. What position did he normally play?
    a) Right back b) Centre back c) Left back

324. How many appearances did he make in total for the club?
    a) 400 b) 500 c) 600

325. How many Premier League titles did he win at the club?
    a) 6 b) 8 c) 10

326. How many international caps did he win?
    a) 45 b) 65 c) 85

327. Who were the opposition for his testimonial match in 2011?
    a) Inter Milan b) Juventus c) Napoli

328. Which TV channel did he join as a pundit after leaving the club?
    a) BT Sport b) ITV Sport c) Sky Sports

329. What was the title of his autobiography?
    a) Red: My Autobiography b) Red: My Life c) Red: My Story

330. What team did he briefly manage?
    a) Espanyol b) Sevilla c) Valencia

Chapter 33: Answers

321. Bury.
322. 5 feet 11 inches.
323. Right back.
324. 400.
325. 8.
326. 85.
327. Juventus.
328. Sky Sports.
329. Red: My Autobiography.
330. Valencia.

Chapter 34: Eric Cantona

331. Where was Cantona born?
    a) Auxerre b) Bordeaux c) Marseille

332. Which club did United buy him from?
    a) Leeds United b) Newcastle United c) West Ham United

333. What transfer fee did United pay for him?
    a) £1.2 million b) £2.2 million c) £3.2 million

334. How many games did he play for United?
    a) 145 b) 165 c) 185

335. How many goals did he score for United?
    a) 62 b) 72 c) 82

336. How many league titles did he win at the club?
    a) 2 b) 3 c) 4

337. When did he win the PFA Players' Player of the Year Award?
    a) 1993-94 b) 1994-95 c) 1995-96

338. Where did he launch a kung-fu kick into the crowd in 1995?
    a) Charlton b) Chelsea c) Crystal Palace

339. What was his nickname?
    a) Entertainer Eric b) King Eric c) Masterful Eric

340. What profession did he move into after retiring from football?
    a) Acting b) Banking c) Insurance

Chapter 34: Cantona Answers

331. Marseille.
332. Leeds United.
333. £1.2 million.
334. 185.
335. 82.
336. 4.
337. 1993/94.
338. Crystal Palace.
339. King Eric.
340. Acting.

Chapter 35: Ryan Giggs

341. Where was Giggs born?
    a) Bridgend b) Cardiff c) Neath

342. What sport was his father a professional sportsman at?
    a) Cricket b) Golf c) Rugby

343. How old was he when he made his debut for United?
    a) 17 b) 18 c) 19

344. How many appearances did he make in total for the club?
    a) 903 b) 933 c) 963

345. How many goals did he score in total for the club?
    a) 148 b) 168 c) 188

346. What was his nickname?
    a) Giggalot b) Giggler c) Giggsy

347. How many Premier League titles did he win at the club?
    a) 9 b) 11 c) 13

348. Who did he score a memorable goal against in the 1999 FA Cup semi final replay?
    a) Arsenal b) Chelsea c) Tottenham Hotspur

349. When did he win the PFA Players' Player of the Year Award?
    a) 2004-05 b) 2006-07 c) 2008-09

350. How old was he when he made his final appearance for United?
    a) 38 b) 39 c) 40

Chapter 35: Answers

341. Cardiff.
342. Rugby, including playing 5 times for Wales.
343. 17.
344. 963.
345. 168.
346. Giggsy.
347. 13.
348. Arsenal. Who could ever forget the goal and the top-off swirling the shirt celebration.
349. 2008-09.
350. 40.

Chapter 36: Cristiano Ronaldo

351. Where was Ronaldo born?
   a) Madeira b) Portugal c) The Azores

352. How tall is he?
   a) 6 feet b) 6 feet 1 inch c) 6 feet 2 inches

353. Which club did United buy him from?
   a) Benfica b) Porto c) Sporting Lisbon

354. What transfer fee did United pay for him?
   a) £10 million b) £11 million c) £12 million

355. How old was he when he made his first team debut?
   a) 17 b) 18 c) 19

356. How many appearances did he make in total for the club?
   a) 212 b) 252 c) 292

357. How many goals did he score for the club?
   a) 98 b) 118 c) 138

358. Which season did he win the Premier League Golden Boot award?
   a) 2006-07 b) 2007-08 c) 2008-09

359. When did he win the Ballon d'Or Award?
   a) 2007 b) 2008 c) 2009

360. Which club did he move to after United?
   a) Barcelona b) Juventus c) Real Madrid

Chapter 36: Answers

351. He was born in Madeira.
352. 6 feet 2 inches tall.
353. Sporting Lisbon.
354. The reported figure was just over £12 million which, at the time, was an English record for a teenager.
355. 18.
356. 292.
357. 118.
358. 2007-08.
359. 2008.
360. Real Madrid.

Chapter 37: Bryan Robson

361. Where was Robson born?
    a) Chester-le-Street b) Chesterfield c) Chichester

362. Which club did United buy him from?
    a) Aston Villa b) WBA c) Wolves

363. What transfer fee did United pay for him?
    a) £500,000 b) £1million c) £1.5 million

364. What was his nickname?
    a) Captain Amazing b) Captain Marvel c) Captain Power

365. How many Premier League titles did he win with United?
    a) 1 b) 2 c) 3

366. How many appearances did he make for United?
    a) 381 b) 421 c) 461

367. How many goals did he score for United?
    a) 79 b) 89 c) 99

368. How many international caps did he win?
    a) 50 b) 70 c) 90

369. Which club did he move to after United?
    a) Bradford City b) Middlesbrough c) Sheffield United

370. Which country did he manage between 2009 and 2011?
    a) Malaysia b) Singapore c) Thailand

Chapter 37: Answers

361. Chester-le-Street in County Durham.
362. WBA.
363. Robson signed for United in October 1981 for a fee of £1.5 million, a British record transfer at the time.
364. Captain Marvel.
365. 2.
366. 461.
367. 99.
368. 90.
369. Middlesbrough.
370. Thailand.

Chapter 38: George Best

371. Where was Best born?
   a) Belfast b) Birkenhead c) Bootle

372. How old was he when he made his first team debut?
   a) 17 b) 18 c) 19

373. How tall was he?
   a) 5 feet 9 inches b) 5 feet 11 inches c) 6 feet 1 inch

374. How many appearances did he make in total for the club?
   a) 370 b) 420 c) 470

375. How many goals did he score for the club?
   a) 119 b) 149 c) 179

376. How many international caps did he win?
   a) 37 b) 57 c) 77

377. How many League titles did he win at the club?
   a) 1 b) 2 c) 3

378. How many clubs did he play for in the North American Soccer League (the fore-runner to MLS)?
   a) 1 b) 2 c) 3

379. How old was he when he died?
   a) 53 b) 56 c) 59

380. What was the title of his autobiography?
   a) Blessed b) Simply The Best c) Wasted

Chapter 38: Answers

371. Belfast.
372. 17.
373. 5 feet 9 inches tall.
374. 470.
375. 179.
376. 37.
377. 2.
378. 3. They were Los Angeles Aztecs, Fort Lauderdale Strikers and San Jose Earthquakes.
379. 59.
380. Blessed.

Chapter 39: Denis Law

381. Where was Law born?
   a) Aberdeen b) Glasgow c) Edinburgh

382. Which club did United buy him from?
   a) Huddersfield Town b) Manchester City c) Torino

383. What transfer fee did United pay for him?
   a) £95,000 b) £105,000 c) £115,000

384. Who did he score against on his United debut?
   a) West Bromwich Albion b) West Ham c) Wolverhampton Wanderers

385. What was his nickname?
   a) The Emperor b) The King c) The Prince

386. How many appearances did he make in total for the club?
   a) 304 b) 404 c) 504

387. How many goals did he score in total for the club?
   a) 207 b) 237 c) 267

388. Who was named after him?
   a) Dennis Bergkamp b) Denis Irwin c) Dennis Wise

389. How many goals did he score for Scotland?
   a) 20 b) 25 c) 30

390. When did he win the Ballon D'Or European Footballer of the Year Award?
   a) 1964 b) 1966 c) 1968

Chapter 39: Answers

381. Aberdeen.
382. Torino.
383. £115,000 which was a British record transfer ta the time.
384. He scored on his debut against West Brom after just 7 minutes.
385. He was nicknamed The King by The United faithful, and was also known as The Lawman and his opponents often called him Denis The Menace.
386. 404.
387. 237.
388. Dennis Bergkamp.
389. He scored 30 goals for Scotland, a joint record.
390. 1964.

Chapter 40: More Nationalities

391. Where was Dimitar Berbatov born?
a) Albania b) Bulgaria c) Romania

392. Where was Anthony Martial born?
a) France b) Italy c) Hungary

393. Where was Ander Herrera born?
a) Serbia b) Slovakia c) Spain

394. Where was Rafael born?
a) Argentina b) Brazil c) Paraguay

395. Where was Robin van Persie born?
a) Belgium b) France c) The Netherlands

396. Where was Nemanja Matic born?
a) Serbia b) Slovakia c) Slovenia

397. Where was Nani born?
a) Brazil b) Chile c) Portugal

398. Where was Juan Mata born?
a) France b) Portugal c) Spain

399. Where was Victor Lindelöf born?
a) Denmark b) Norway c) Sweden

400. Where was Dwight York born?
a) Ivory Coast b) Senegal c) Trinidad and Tobago

Chapter 40: Answers

391. Berbatov was born in Bulgaria.
392. Martial was born in France.
393. Herrera was born in Spain.
394. Rafael was born in Brazil.
395. van Persie was born in The Netherlands.
396. Matic was born in Serbia.
397. Nani was born in Portugal.
398. Mata was born in Spain.
399. Lindelöf was born in Sweden.
400. Yorke was born in Trinidad and Tobago.

Chapter 41: More Shirt Numbers

401. What shirt number is associated with Marcus Rashford?
    a) 10 b) 12 c) 14

402. What shirt number is associated with Ashley Young?
    a) 14 b) 16 c) 18

403. What shirt number is associated with Arthur Albiston?
    a) 3 b) 13 c) 23

404. What shirt number is associated with Wes Brown?
    a) 2 b) 3 c) 6

405 What shirt number is associated with Jesse Lingard?
    a) 14 b) 15 c) 16

406. What shirt number is associated with Rio Ferdinand?
    a) 3 b) 4 c) 5

407. What shirt number is associated with Antonio Valencia?
    a) 23 b) 25 c) 27

408. What shirt number is associated with Dimitar Berbatov?
    a) 7 b) 8 c) 9

409. What shirt number is associated with Steve Bruce?
    a) 4 b) 8 c) 11

410. What shirt number is associated with Nemanja Vidic?
    a) 5 b) 15 c) 25

Chapter 41: Answers

401. Rashford – 10.
402. Young – 18.
403. Albiston – 3.
404. Brown – 6.
405. Lingard – 14.
406. Ferdinand – 5.
407. Valencia – 25.
408. Berbatov – 9.
409. Bruce – 4.
410. Vidic – 15.

Chapter 42: 1960s Transfers

411. Which club was Noel Cantwell signed from in 1960?
 a) Leeds United b) Newcastle United c) West Ham United

412. Which club was David Herd signed from in 1961?
 a) Arsenal b) Stockport County c) Stoke City

413. Which club was Pat Crerand signed from in 1963?
 a) Aberdeen b) Celtic c) Rangers

414. Which club was Johnny Giles sold to in 1963?
 a) Leeds United b) Liverpool c) WBA

415. Which club was John Connelly signed from in 1964?
 a) Blackburn Rovers b) Burnley c) Bury

416. Which club was Pat Dunne signed from in 1964?
 a) Bray Wanderers b) Dundalk c) Shamrock Rovers

417. How much was Maurice Setters sold to Stoke City for in 1964?
 a) £10,000 b) £30,000 c) £50,000

418. Which club was Alex Stepney signed from in 1966?
 a) Arsenal b) Chelsea c) West Ham United

419. Which club was Harry Gregg sold to in 1966?
 a) Coventry City b) Leicester City c) Stoke City

420. Which club was Willie Morgan signed from in 1968?
 a) Blackpool b) Bolton Wanderers c) Burnley

Chapter 42: Answers

411. West Ham United.
412. Arsenal.
413. Celtic.
414. Leeds United.
415. Burnley.
416. Shamrock Rovers.
417. £30,000.
418. Chelsea.
419. Stoke City.
420. Burnley.

Chapter 43: 1970s Transfers

421. Which club was Nobby Stiles sold to in 1971?
   a) Mansfield b) Middlesbrough c) Millwall

422. Who did the club sign from Nottingham Forest in 1972?
   a) Wyn Davies b) Ted McDougall c) Ian Storey-Moore

423. Which club was Big Jim Holton bought from in 1973?
   a) Shrewsbury Town b) Sunderland c) Swansea City

424. Which club was Stewart Houston bought from in 1973?
   a) Arsenal b) Brentford c) Sheffield United

425. Which club was Lou Macari bought from in 1973?
   a) Chelsea b) Celtic c) Crystal Palace

426. Which club was Stuart Pearson bought from in 1974?
   a) Cardiff City b) Hull City c) Lincoln City

427. Which club was Steve Coppell bought from in 1975?
   a) Blackburn Rovers b) Bristol Rovers c) Tranmere Rovers

428. Which club was Jimmy Greenhoff bought from in 1976?
   a) Birmingham City b) Coventry City c) Stoke City

429. How much did Gordon McQueen cost when joining from Leeds United in 1978?
   a) £300,000 b) £500,000 c) £700,000

430. Which club was Ray Wilkins bought from in 1979?
   a) Chelsea b) QPR c) Rangers

Chapter 43: Answers

421. Middlesbrough.
422. Ian Storey-Moore.
423. Shrewsbury Town.
424. Brentford.
425. Celtic.
426. Hull City.
427. Tranmere Rovers.
428. Stoke City.
429. £500,000.
430. Chelsea.

Chapter 44: 1980s Transfers

431. Which club was Remi Moses bought from in 1981?
    a) Aston Villa b) Birmingham City c) West Bromwich Albion

432. What was the transfer fee paid to St Patrick's Athletic for Paul McGrath in 1982?
    a) £30,000 b) £130,000 c) £230,000

433. Which club was Frank Stapleton bought from in 1981?
    a) Ajax b) Anderlecht c) Arsenal

434. Which club was Joe Jordan sold to in 1982?
    a) AC Milan b) Juventus c) Roma

435. Which club was Jesper Olsen bought from in 1984?
    a) Ajax b) Anderlecht c) Arsenal

436. Which club was Brian McClair bought from in 1987?
    a) Ayr United b) Celtic c) Dundee

437. How much did Steve Bruce cost when he joined United in 1987?
    a) £700,000 b) £800,000 c) £900,000

438. Which club was Lee Sharpe bought from in 1988?
    a) Leeds United b) Newcastle United c) Torquay United

439. How much did Mark Hughes cost when re-joining from Barcelona in 1988?
    a) £1.2 million b) £1.5 million c) £1.8 million

440. Which club was Gary Pallister bought from in 1989?
    a) Middlesbrough b) Sheffield United c) Stoke City

Chapter 44: Answers

431. WBA.
432. £30,000.
433. Arsenal.
434. AC Milan.
435. Ajax.
436. Celtic.
437. £800,000.
438. Torquay United.
439. £1.8 million which was a club record transfer at the time.
440. Middlesbrough.

Chapter 45: 1990s Transfers

441. Which club was Deni Irwin bought from in 1990?
    a) Leeds United b) Oldham Athletic c) Wolverhampton Wanderers

442. What was the transfer fee paid to Brondby for Peter Schmeichel in 1991?
    a) £305,000 b) £505,000 c) £705,000

443. Which club was Andrei Kanchelskis bought from in 1991?
    a) Dynamo Kiev b) Krylia Sovetov c) Shaktar Donetsk

444. Which club was Andy Cole bought from in 1995?
    a) Blackburn Rovers b) Fulham c) Newcastle United

445. How much was Mark Hughes sold to Chelsea for in 1995?
    a) £1 million b) £2 million c) £3 million

446. Which club was Teddy Sheringham bought from in 1997?
    a) Nottingham Forest b) Portsmouth c) Tottenham Hotspur

447. Which club was Jaap Stam bought from in 1998?
    a) Lazio b) PSV Eindhoven c) Willem II

448. Which club was Dwight Yorke bought from in 1998?
    a) Aston Villa b) Birmingham City c) Blackburn Rovers

449. Which club was Quinton Fortune bought from in 1999?
    a) Atletico Madrid b) Barcelona c) Real Madrid

450. Which club was Mikael Silvestre bought from in 1999?
    a) Inter Milan b) Rennes c) Werder Bremen

Chapter 45: Answers

441. Monaco.
442. £28.1 million, which was a record transfer in English football at the time
443. PSV Eindhoven.
444. Leeds United.
445. Real Madrid.
446. Newcastle United.
447. Spartak Moscow.
448. Monaco.
449. Edwin van der Saar.
450. Tottenham Hotspur.

Chapter 46: 2000-2009 Transfers

451. Which club was Fabien Barthez bought from in 2000?
    a) Marseille b) Monaco c) Toulouse

452. What was the transfer fee paid to Lazio for Juan Sebastian Veron in 2001?
    a) £22.1 million b) £25.1 million c) £28.1 million

453. Which club was Diego Forlan bought from in 2002?
    a) Boca Juniors b) Independiente c) River Plate

454. Which club was Rio Ferdinand bought from in 2002?
    a) Leeds United b) Newcastle United c) West Ham United

455. Which club was David Beckham sold to in 2003?
    a) Real Betis b) Real Madrid c) Real Sociedad

456. Which club was Nicky Butt sold to in 2004?
    a) Birmingham City b) Newcastle United c) Southampton

457. Which club was Nemanja Vidic bought from in 2006?
    a) Inter Milan b) Red Star Belgrade c) Spartak Moscow

458. Which club was Patrice Evra bought from in 2006?
    a) Marseille b) Monaco c) Monza

459. Which goalkeeper was bought from Fulham in 2006?
    a) Mark Bosnich b) Ben Foster c) Edwin van der Sar

460. Which club was Michael Carrick bought from in 2006?
    a) Arsenal b) Tottenham Hotspur c) West Ham United

Chapter 46: Answers

451. Leicester City.
452. Coventry City.
453. Independiente.
454. Monaco.
455. Leeds United.
456. Real Sociedad.
457. Luis Garcia.
458. Villareal.
459. Feyenoord
460. Zenit St Petersburg.

Chapter 47: 2010-2020 Transfers

461. Who was bought from Guadalajara in 2010?
    a) Javier Hernandez b) Marcos Rojo c) Alexis Sanchez

462. Which club was Chris Smalling bought from in 2010?
    a) Charlton b) Fulham c) Millwall

463. Which club was John O'Shea sold to in 2011?
    a) Middlesbrough b) Newcastle United c) Sunderland

464. Which club did United sign David de Gea from in 2011?
    a) Athletic Bilbao b) Atletico Levante c) Atletico Madrid

465. Which club did United sign Ashley Young from in 2011?
    a) Aston Villa b) Inter Milan c) Watford

466. What fee did United get for Paul Pogba when he went to Juventus in 2012?
    a) £0 b) £25 million c) £50 million

467. Which club did United sign Juan Mata from in 2014?
    a) Arsenal b) Chelsea c) Manchester City

468. Which club did United sign Luke Shaw from in 2014?
    a) Sheffield United b) Southampton c) Swansea City

469. Which club did United sign Anthony Martial from in 2015?
    a) Lille b) Monaco c) Toulouse

470. Which club did United sign Romelu Lukaku from in 2017?
    a) Chelsea b) Everton c) WBA

Chapter 47: Answers

461. Javier Hernandez, who is also known as Chicarito.
462. Fulham.
463. Sunderland.
464. Atletico Madrid.
465. Aston Villa.
466. £0. Juventus made a good profit when he was sold back to United 4 years later.
467. Chelsea.
468. Southampton.
469. Monaco.
470. Everton.

Chapter 48: Charity/Community Shield

471. How many times have United won the Charity/Community Shield?
    a) 17 b) 19 c) 21

472. Who did United beat in the 2016 Community Shield?
    a) Chelsea b) Leicester City c) Manchester City

473. Who did United beat in the 2013 Community Shield?
    a) Arsenal b) Chelsea c) Wigan Athletic

474. What score did United beat Manchester City in the 2011 Community Shield?
    a) 1-0 b) 2-1 c) 3-2

475. Who did United beat in the 2010 Community Shield?
    a) Arsenal b) Chelsea c) Portsmouth

476. What score did United beat Newcastle United in the 1996 Charity Shield?
    a) 2-0 b) 3-0 c) 4-0

477. What score did United beat Blackburn Rovers in the 1994 Charity Shield?
    a) 2-0 b) 3-0 c) 4-0

478. Who did United beat in the 1983 Charity Shield?
    a) Everton b) Liverpool c) Tottenham Hotspur

479. What score did United beat Aston Villa in the 1957 Charity Shield?
    a) 2-0 b) 3-0 c) 4-0

480. Who did United beat in the first ever Charity Shield in 1908?
    a) Newcastle United b) Queens Park Rangers c) Swindon Town

Chapter 48: Answers

471. United have won a record 21 Charity/Community Shields in total. 17 outright victories and 4 shard.
472. Leicester City.
473. Wigan Athletic.
474. 3-2.
475. Chelsea.
476. 4-0.
477. 2-0.
478. Liverpool
479. 4-0.
480. Queens Park Rangers.

Chapter 49: Sir Bobby Charlton

481. Where was Sir Bobby born?
    a) Northamptonshire b) Northumberland c) Nottinghamshire

482. How tall is he?
    a) 5 feet 6 inches b) 5 feet 8 inches c) 5 feet 10 inches

483. How old was he when he made his first team debut for United?
    a) 18 b) 19 c) 20

484. How many appearances did he make in total for the club?
    a) 558 b) 658 c) 758

485. How many goals did he score for United?
    a) 209 b) 229 c) 249

486. How many times was he capped for England?
    a) 102 b) 104 c) 106

487. How many goals did he score for England?
    a) 41 b) 45 c) 49

488. When did he win the Football Writers Association Player of the Year Award?
    a) 1964-65 b) 1965-66 c) 1966-67

489. When did he win the Ballon D'Or European Footballer of the Year Award?
    a) 1964 b) 1966 c) 1968

490. When was he knighted?
    a) 1990 b) 1994 c) 1998

Chapter 49: Answers

481. He was born in the small mining town of Ashington in Northumberland.
482. 5 feet 8 inches.
483. He made his debut aged 18, just a week before his 19th birthday.
484. 758.
485. 249.
486. 106.
487. 49.
488. 1965-6.
489. 1966.
490. 1994.

Chapter 50: Sir Alex Ferguson

491. Where was Ferguson born?
    a) Dundee b) Edinburgh c) Glasgow

492. What position did he play during his playing career?
    a) Defence b) Midfield c) Attack

493. How tall is he?
    a) 5 feet 9 inches b) 5 feet 10 inches c) 5 feet 11 inches

494. Who did he manage just before coming to United?
    a) Aberdeen b) Celtic c) Rangers

495. What year did he become manager of United?
    a) 1984 b) 1985 c) 1986

496. Who was his first signing for United?
    a) Viv Anderson b) Jim Leighton c) Brian McClair

497. Where did the club finish at the end of his first season in charge?
    a) 5th b) 8th c) 11th

498. How many games was he in charge of United?
    a) 1300 b) 1400 c) 1500

499. How many Premier League titles did United win in total under Sir Alex?
    a) 11 b) 12 c) 13

500. How many major trophies did United win in total under Sir Alex?
    a) 28 b) 33 c) 38

Chapter 50: Answers

491. Glasgow.
492. Attack.
493. 5 feet 11 inches.
494. Aberdeen.
495. 1986.
496. Viv Anderson.
497. 11th.
498. 1500.
499. 13.
500. 38. Thank you Sir Alex for all you did for the club.

Helping One Another

That's it. I hope you enjoyed the book and if you did, would you please leave a helpful review of it on Amazon. All reviews are very much appreciated.

If you have any comments, or ideas for improvements to this book, you can contact me at conan@johnandcel.co.uk and I will do my best to reply to your message, as I read every email.

Your review and message is important, and this book has already been revised and improved thanks to suggestions from other fans.

Many thanks in advance

Conan.

Printed in Great Britain
by Amazon